High Spirits!

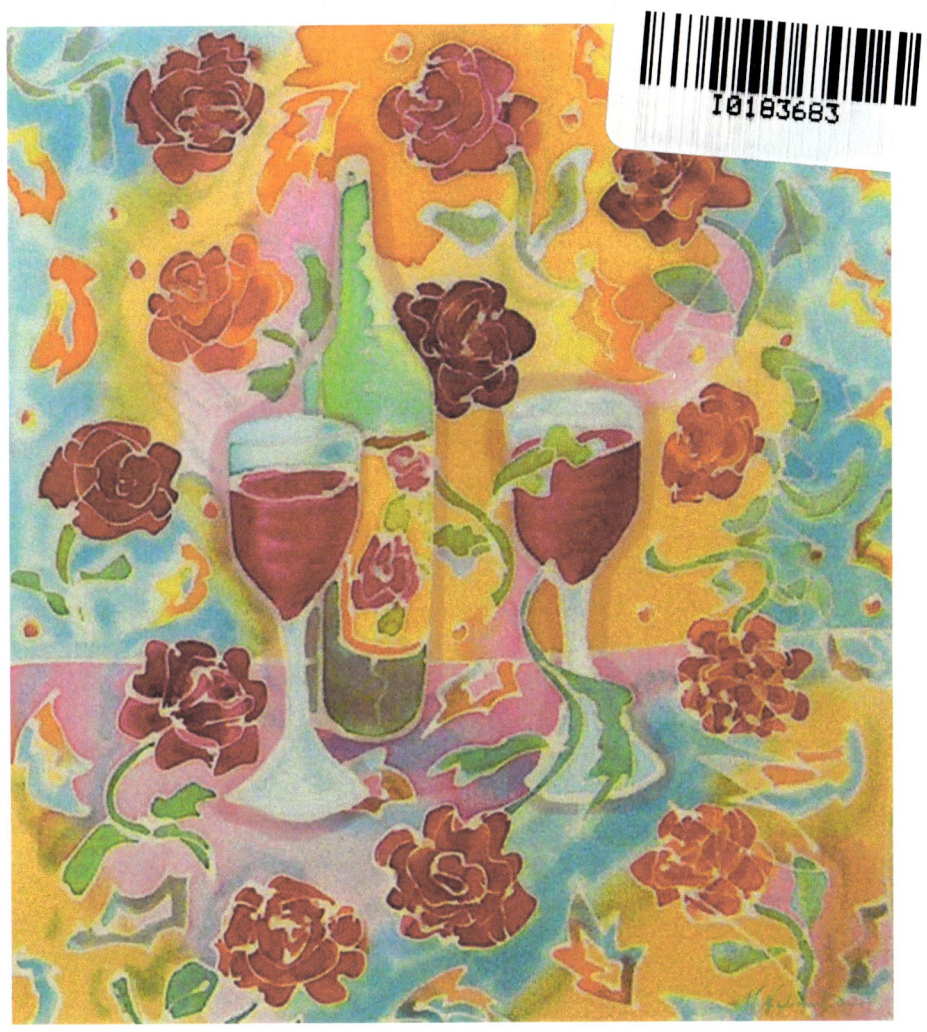

by M. Nicole van Dam

An Artimagination® Book Blending Fine Art & Inspiration

We hope that You enjoy this Artimagination® Book of Fine Art and Inspiration by *M. Nicole van Dam.*

M. Nicole van Dam is an internationally licensed artist/designer, as well as a published author of several adult books such as [Tempo – The Rhythm and Rhyme of the Artist](#) and several children's books, including [Inca Dink, the Great Houndini](#) (which she also illustrated). Nicole's work has a distinctive center that engages and charms. A California native born of Dutch immigrant parents, Nicole's work expresses West Coast and European influences, and celebrates the beauty and diversity of the California Central Coast and North East seasons.

Thank You for supporting the artwork and creativity of M. Nicole van Dam. We look forward to hearing Your thoughts.

This book is an Artimagination® imprint. To contact Artimagination about this work or the author:

High Spirits! by M. Nicole van Dam
P.O. Box 583
Ojai, CA 93024

Email: Nicole@Artimagination.com
Website: [Artimagination.com](#)
Blog: [Wishes.bz](#)

Trademark and Copyright © 2014 by M. Nicole van Dam. All Rights Reserved. No part of this book may be used or reproduced in any manner whatsoever without the express written permission of the Author and Artist, M. Nicole van Dam.

Accomplishment is Champagne for the soul

(M. Nicole van Dam)

Artwork: "High Spirits!" by M. Nicole van Dam

What you get by achieving your goals is not as important as what you become by achieving your goals.

(Goethe)

Artwork: "On the Set" by M. Nicole van Dam

The gift you give yourself is trying.

(M. Nicole van Dam)

Artwork: "Leap of Faith" by M. Nicole van Dam

Strive and Thrive

(M. Nicole van Dam)

Artwork: "Rat Race" by M. Nicole van Dam

Life is an Adventure – or it is nothing

(Helen Keller)

Artwork: "California Gold" by M. Nicole van Dam

As the circle of light increases, so does the circumference of darkness around it

(Albert Einstein)

Artwork: "Yellow Light" by M. Nicole van Dam

We can't always choose what life gives us to paint, but we get to choose the colors.

(M. Nicole van Dam)

Artwork: "Sailing" by M. Nicole van Dam

Dare

Don't let your past own today

Don't sell today for the morrow

Don't mortgage your future

Pine not for a past only borrowed

Don't fear laughing, loving or living

Never forget the joy of sharing, caring and giving

Fear not the sorrow of loss

of a soul tempest tossed

Live fully

Set the you of you free

To strive, to shine

Be all that you dare to be.

(M. Nicole van Dam)

Artwork: "It's Spring" by M. Nicole van Dam

Faith in Time

The Universe brings you what you are to get
And though more often than not,
I fret

That it's not what I want
Not what I wish
Not that which makes my heart soar

With patience
Open-mindedness
Open heart
I see, in time,

That the Universe gave me
much more.

(M. Nicole van Dam)

Artwork: "Moon" by M. Nicole van Dam

Creativity is wondrous in all its forms – find your own song to sing, and let your heart smile in harmony when others find theirs.

(M. Nicole van Dam)

Artwork: "Cello Fantasy" by M. Nicole van Dam

Don this mask and become a stranger,
   an unknown guest

Mirrored in others' eyes, the question,

Are you villain, hero, observer, or in conquest?

Here is your visage for adventure and treasure untold

Embark upon this masquerade journey,

Let the Voyage unfold!

(M. Nicole van Dam)

Artwork: "Masquerade" by M. Nicole van Dam

It took Edison more than 1800 tries before he found a light bulb design that worked.

Artwork: "Sun" by M. Nicole van Dam

Believe and be alive

(M. Nicole van Dam)

Artwork: "Pansy" by M. Nicole van Dam

If at first you don't succeed, try try try try try try try try try try try try try try try try again.
Repeat as needed.

(M. Nicole van Dam)

Artwork: "Cats and a World to Explore" by M. Nicole van Dam

Failure is evidence that you tried;
Success is evidence that you tried harder.

(M. Nicole van Dam)

Artwork: "Roses of Conquest" by M. Nicole van Dam

The best way to get anything done is to do.

(M. Nicole van Dam)

Artwork: "Ballet des Fleurs" by M. Nicole van Dam

Sometimes it <u>is</u> hard to keep trying;
Sometimes it <u>is</u> hard to keep believing.
That's when you need to ask yourself:
When you are 100 and look back on this moment, what do you want to see?

(M. Nicole van Dam)

Artwork: "Meubles des Jardin" by M. Nicole van Dam

There is always hope as long as you keep trying

Artwork: "There is Always Hope" by M. Nicole van Dam

It's not what life throws you, it's how you fetch the ball.

(M. Nicole van Dam)

Artwork: "Fetch" by M. Nicole van Dam

Toughen up, buck up, and get back to work!

Artwork: "The Catch" by M. Nicole van Dam

The only thing you get by continually looking back is a sore neck.

(M. Nicole van Dam)

Artwork: "The Glance" by M. Nicole van Dam

The lessons learned on the path to success are your mind's nourishment for the next step.

(M. Nicole van Dam)

Artwork: "Tea Time" by M. Nicole van Dam

If it was easy, everybody would do it.

Artwork: "Of Mice and Music" painted violin by M. Nicole van Dam

Attitude will bring you altitude.

(M. Nicole van Dam)

Artwork: "Lake of Dreams" by M. Nicole van Dam

Undiscovered dreams
An unexpected journey
Drifting along memories and hopes
A sweet yearning
Of what could be
Should be
May still
All there for my eye to see
In this painting on the wall.

(M. Nicole van Dam)

Artwork: "Gondolier of Venice" by M. Nicole van Dam

The best antidote for depression is to give your brain the treat of learning something new.

(M. Nicole van Dam)

Artwork: "The Letter A" by M. Nicole van Dam

*It takes a lot of effort to beat yourself up.
You might as well use all that effort to learn something
new and to try once more.*

(M. Nicole van Dam)

Artwork: "Reading Leonberger Dog" by M. Nicole van Dam

Your biggest critic, your biggest hurdle, is that voice within you that says you won't be able to accomplish things. I have never met anyone who doesn't hear that voice. Just remember that the reward of giving your dream a chance is far greater than the reward of proving your negative self correct.

(M. Nicole van Dam)
Artwork: "The Jester" by M. Nicole van Dam

Pursuing your dream is like a fine wine – it gets better as it evolves through time.

(M. Nicole van Dam)

Artwork: "The Bounty of Grapes" by M. Nicole van Dam

Thank You for supporting the artwork and creativity of M. Nicole van Dam. We hope that You enjoy this Book, and look forward to hearing Your thoughts.

TO CONTACT NICOLE:

M. Nicole van Dam
 P.O. Box 583
Ojai, CA 93024

Email: Nicole@Artimagination.com
Website: Create.bz
Blog: Nicole.bz

On the Cover:

HIGH SPIRITS!
By M. Nicole van Dam

Dedication

This Book is dedicated to my Mother and Father, who through their support and belief in me gave me a safe bridge to a new life, and to my husband Jay, who is my new life.

Books featuring the Works of
M. Nicole van Dam:

Tempo – The Rhythm & Rhyme of the Artist

High Spirits!

M. Nicole van Dam, a Retrospective 2010

Inca Dink, The Great Houndini

Rosie and Emma Plant a Seed
This Little Puppy

The Background Story of Inca Dink, The Great HOundini

To learn more, please visit Wishes.bz

www.ingramcontent.com/pod-product-compliance
Lightning Source LLC
LaVergne TN
LVHW010018070426
835512LV00001B/13